THIS WALKER BOOK BELONGS TO:

Mrs. Macdonald

For Wendy and Matthew

First published 1991
by Walker Books Ltd
87 Vauxhall Walk
London SE11 5HJ

This edition published 1994

10 9 8 7 6 5 4 3 2 1

© 1991 Marcia Williams

Printed in Hong Kong

British Library Cataloguing in Publication Data
A catalogue record for this book is
available from the British Library.

ISBN 0-7445-3075-X

GREEK MYTHS

for young children

MARCIA WILLIAMS

WALKER BOOKS

LONDON

PANDORA'S BOX

In the beginning, the gods lived on Mount Olympus.

But only giants and wild beasts lived on earth.

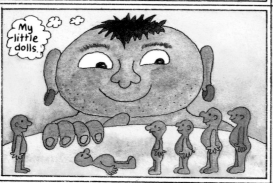

Then the giant Prometheus made people out of clay

and Zeus breathed life into them.

Prometheus taught mankind all he knew,

including respect for the gods.

Zeus occasionally sent a thunderbolt hurtling to earth to remind mankind of his power,

but otherwise, harmony reigned …

until Prometheus played a trick on Zeus.

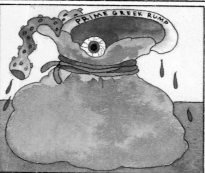

Confused as to how to offer a sacrificial bull to Zeus, some men asked Prometheus to show them what to do.

He put a steak on top of one sack of guts and eyeballs.

Then he put guts on top of a sack of chops and steak.

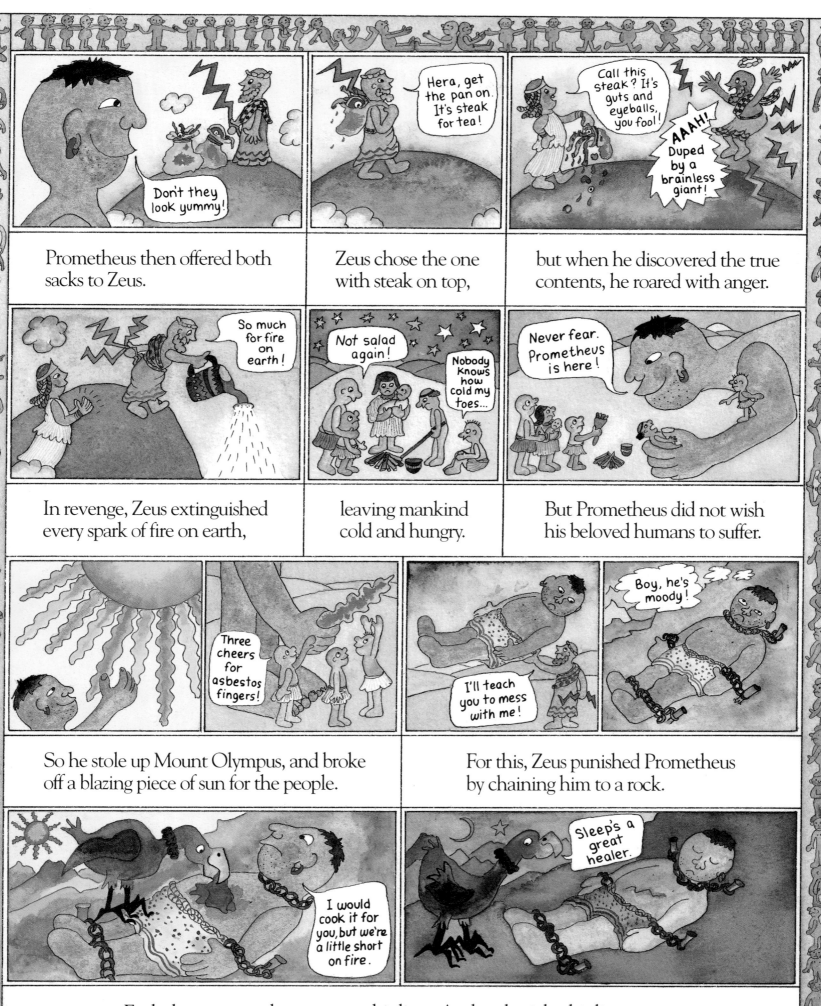

Prometheus then offered both sacks to Zeus.

Zeus chose the one with steak on top,

but when he discovered the true contents, he roared with anger.

In revenge, Zeus extinguished every spark of fire on earth,

leaving mankind cold and hungry.

But Prometheus did not wish his beloved humans to suffer.

So he stole up Mount Olympus, and broke off a blazing piece of sun for the people.

For this, Zeus punished Prometheus by chaining him to a rock.

Each day a great vulture tore out his liver. And each night, his liver grew again. The torture continued for months before Prometheus was released.

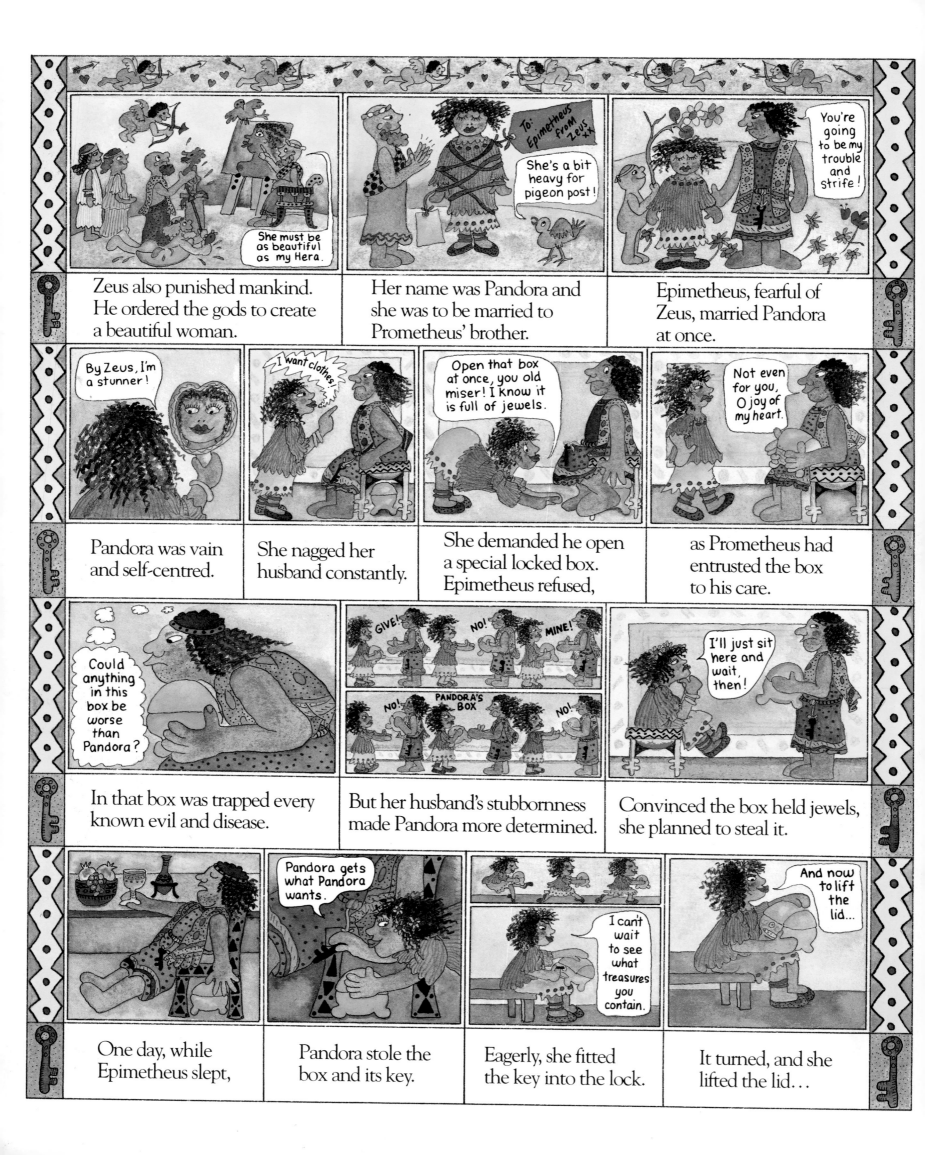

Zeus also punished mankind. He ordered the gods to create a beautiful woman.

Her name was Pandora and she was to be married to Prometheus' brother.

Epimetheus, fearful of Zeus, married Pandora at once.

Pandora was vain and self-centred.

She nagged her husband constantly.

She demanded he open a special locked box. Epimetheus refused,

as Prometheus had entrusted the box to his care.

In that box was trapped every known evil and disease.

But her husband's stubbornness made Pandora more determined.

Convinced the box held jewels, she planned to steal it.

One day, while Epimetheus slept,

Pandora stole the box and its key.

Eagerly, she fitted the key into the lock.

It turned, and she lifted the lid...

All at once, every evil and spite flew out, like a swarm of insects, covering Pandora and infesting the earth with pain and sorrow.

Luckily, Prometheus had also locked "hope" in the box, so mankind was saved from total despair. But – thanks to Pandora – life on earth was never quite so joyful again.

ARION AND THE DOLPHINS

Like most Greeks, Periander, King of Corinth, was a music lover.

His court was crowded with singers and musicians.

But his favourite star was Arion. Arion's music always put Periander in a good mood.

So when Arion asked to visit Sicily for a music festival, Periander hated the idea.

"I shall be out of humour all the time you're away," he declared gloomily.

Finally Arion convinced him that it would be worth all the prize money he would win.

So a ship was rigged and manned and Arion set sail for Sicily.

Once there, it seemed that Arion could not play or sing a wrong note.

He won so many prizes that it took twelve porters to carry them to the ship.

Arion was delighted to be returning home to Periander with such fame and fortune.

The sailors were delighted too, for they had a mind to steal the prizes.

When the ship was well out to sea, they surrounded Arion with shouts of, "You must die!"

Arion tried to persuade them to take his gold and spare his life.

But the sailors felt they would only be safe with Arion dead.

Arion pleaded to be allowed to sing one last song.

He knelt on the prow and sang to the gods to look on him kindly.

Then, as the last notes died away, he threw himself into the sea.

The waves closed over him and the ship sailed on.

Arion's beautiful singing attracted a school of dolphins who took him to the shores of Corinth.

Arriving home before the ship, Arion related his adventures to Periander.

Relieved to have Arion back, Periander swore to punish the sailors.

Upon their return, Periander hid Arion behind a screen before summoning the sailors.

"Have you news of Arion?" Periander asked. "Why, yes," the sailors replied. "He has been delayed in Sicily by all the festivities."

As they spoke these words, Arion appeared from behind the screen.

The sailors tried to run away but the guards surrounded them.

Periander was all for having the murderous thieves executed on the spot,

but Arion was more merciful and begged that they be allowed to live.

So Periander banished them to an ugly, barbarous land.

This done, Periander settled back to enjoy some of Arion's finest singing.

As the music floated around him, Periander's thoughts grew calm and, for the first time since Arion's departure, a smile came to his lips.

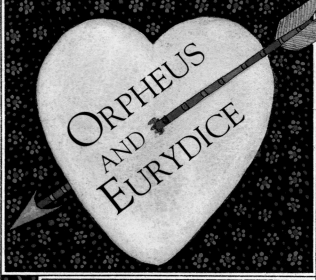

ORPHEUS AND EURYDICE

Orpheus was a famous poet and musician. People came from all over Greece to hear him play his lyre and sing.

His music made wild beasts tame, and trees bend to listen.

Orpheus loved the beautiful nymph, Eurydice. The day they married was the happiest in his life.

Eurydice loved dancing and often went to romp in the fields. But one day, dancing among the meadow flowers, she trod upon a deadly snake.

The snake sank its poisonous fangs into her ankle. Eurydice, overcome by the fatal poison, died instantly.

Orpheus, when he heard the news, was inconsolable and for days
would neither eat nor drink. His friends feared for his life.

Then, without a word, he took his lyre and left the house. He travelled to
Hades, the land of the dead, to beg for the return of his beloved Eurydice.

At last he came to the River Styx, on the edge of the underworld,
where Charon, the ferryman, waited to carry the dead across.

At first Charon refused to
take the living Orpheus.

But when Orpheus played to him
upon his lyre, Charon relented.

On the other side of the river, Orpheus' journey became a nightmare.

First he had to travel through the asphodel fields –
fields that were dark and grey and haunted by ghosts.

Then on he went through Tartarus, where the evil were tortured and
where the guard-dog, Cerberus, growled and snapped at his heels.

Finally, Orpheus reached the centre. He knelt before King Pluto and his queen, Persephone,
who were amazed that a living person should risk his life to reach their kingdom.

Orpheus then took up his lyre and sang of his love for Eurydice
and of his great sorrow. Pluto and Persephone were moved to tears.

They agreed to release Eurydice, on one condition:

Orpheus was not to look back until he reached the world of the living.
So Orpheus departed, without knowing whether Eurydice followed or not.

As he came to the River Styx, he hesitated: if Pluto and Persephone
had tricked him, this was his last chance to go back.

With one foot in the boat, Orpheus turned –
and saw his beloved Eurydice, smiling upon him.

But then her living form faded and Eurydice
became a ghost of the underworld.

And as Charon slowly ferried him into the sunlit world, Orpheus
realized that this time he had lost his love for ever.

THE TWELVE TASKS OF HERACLES

Heracles was a tough little baby.

Everyone loved him but Hera, Zeus' wife, who sent two snakes to kill him.

But Heracles strangled both of them.

For a while, Hera ignored Heracles.

As he grew up, Heracles became stronger and stronger and stronger.

He married and had many children.

Hera hated him being so happy.

So one night she put a spell on him. He lashed out with his sword, killing imaginary enemies.

But when he woke, he saw he had killed his own children.

Heart-broken, Heracles went to the temple to seek forgiveness.

The priestess said he could make amends by serving his old enemy, King Eurystheus.

The King was frightened of Heracles, so he hid in a pot whenever he came near.

And because he hated Heracles, he gave him twelve deadly tasks.

First, Heracles had to kill a huge lion whose hide was so thick that no sword could penetrate it.

Next, he had to kill the many-headed Hydra, whose very breath could kill man or beast.

Thirdly, he had to capture the sacred, golden-horned deer, an animal as quick as the wind.

The fourth task was to catch a savage boar whose tusks could pierce any armour.

Next, Heracles had to clean out, in one night, the vast and filthy stables of King Augeas.

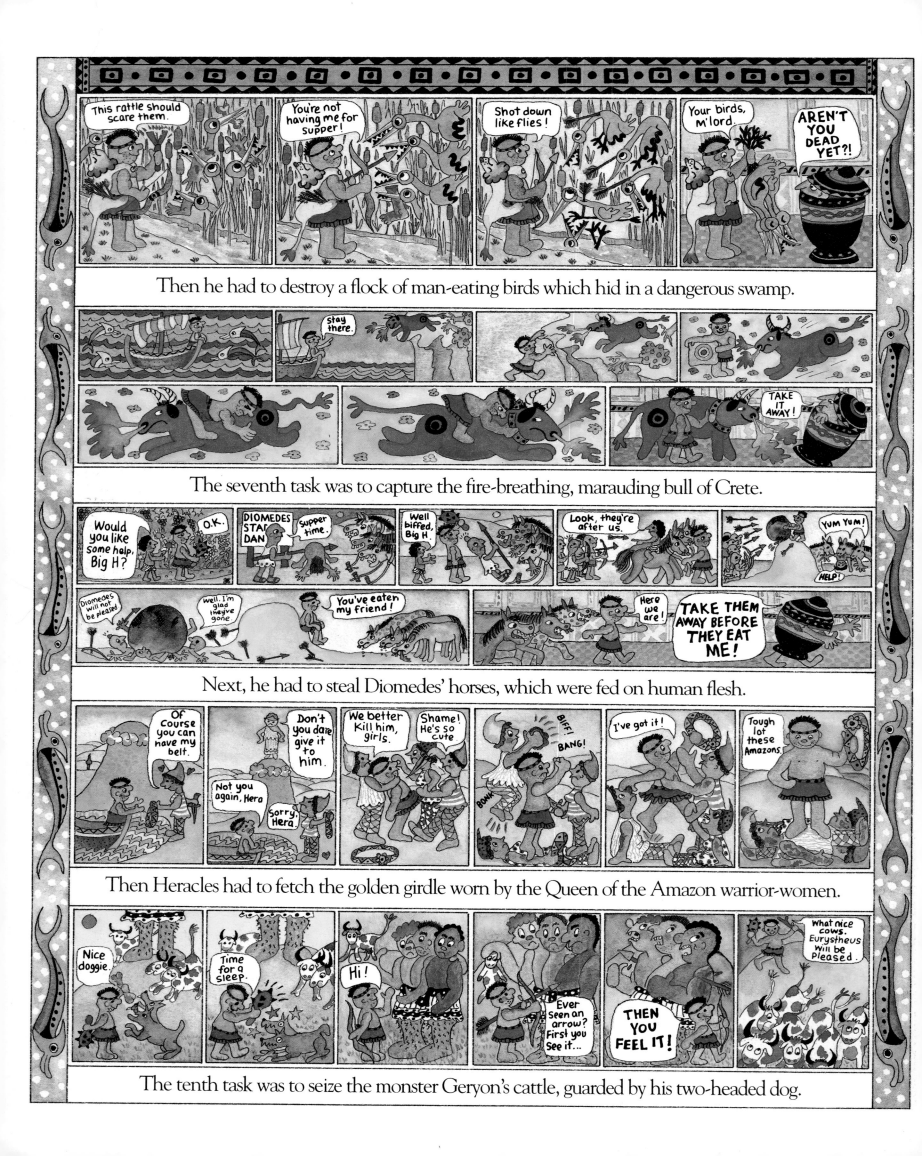

Then he had to destroy a flock of man-eating birds which hid in a dangerous swamp.

The seventh task was to capture the fire-breathing, marauding bull of Crete.

Next, he had to steal Diomedes' horses, which were fed on human flesh.

Then Heracles had to fetch the golden girdle worn by the Queen of the Amazon warrior-women.

The tenth task was to seize the monster Geryon's cattle, guarded by his two-headed dog.

The eleventh, to collect three golden apples protected by a ferocious dragon.

Heracles' twelfth and last task was the most dangerous of all: to fetch the three-headed guard dog, Cerberus, from Hell itself.

His twelve tasks completed, Heracles returned to King Eurystheus.

The King was dismayed to see him alive, and quickly sent him packing.

Then, to avoid angering the gods, Heracles sent Cerberus back to Hades.

At the temple, Heracles was finally pardoned.

He was content at last, and stronger than ever!

And Hera never bothered Heracles again.

DAEDALUS AND ICARUS

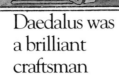

Daedalus was a brilliant craftsman

who worked for the King of Athens.

The statues Daedalus made looked so real that people believed they could talk.

He had a nephew, Talos, who was his apprentice.

Talos was a clever boy. He invented the saw, the compass and the potter's wheel.

But Daedalus was jealous of his nephew's talent and pushed Talos from the roof of the temple.

The goddess Athene, seeing Talos fall, turned him into a partridge, which flew away.

But Talos' body lay crushed on the ground, and Daedalus feared punishment.

So, with his son Icarus, he fled to Crete, where King Minos welcomed him.

Daedalus made many beautiful statues and temples, furniture and vessels for King Minos.

He also made the Labyrinth, a confusing maze of passages where the man-eating Minotaur lived.

King Minos was afraid that Daedalus might reveal the secret way in and out of the Labyrinth,

so he imprisoned Daedalus and his son on the island.

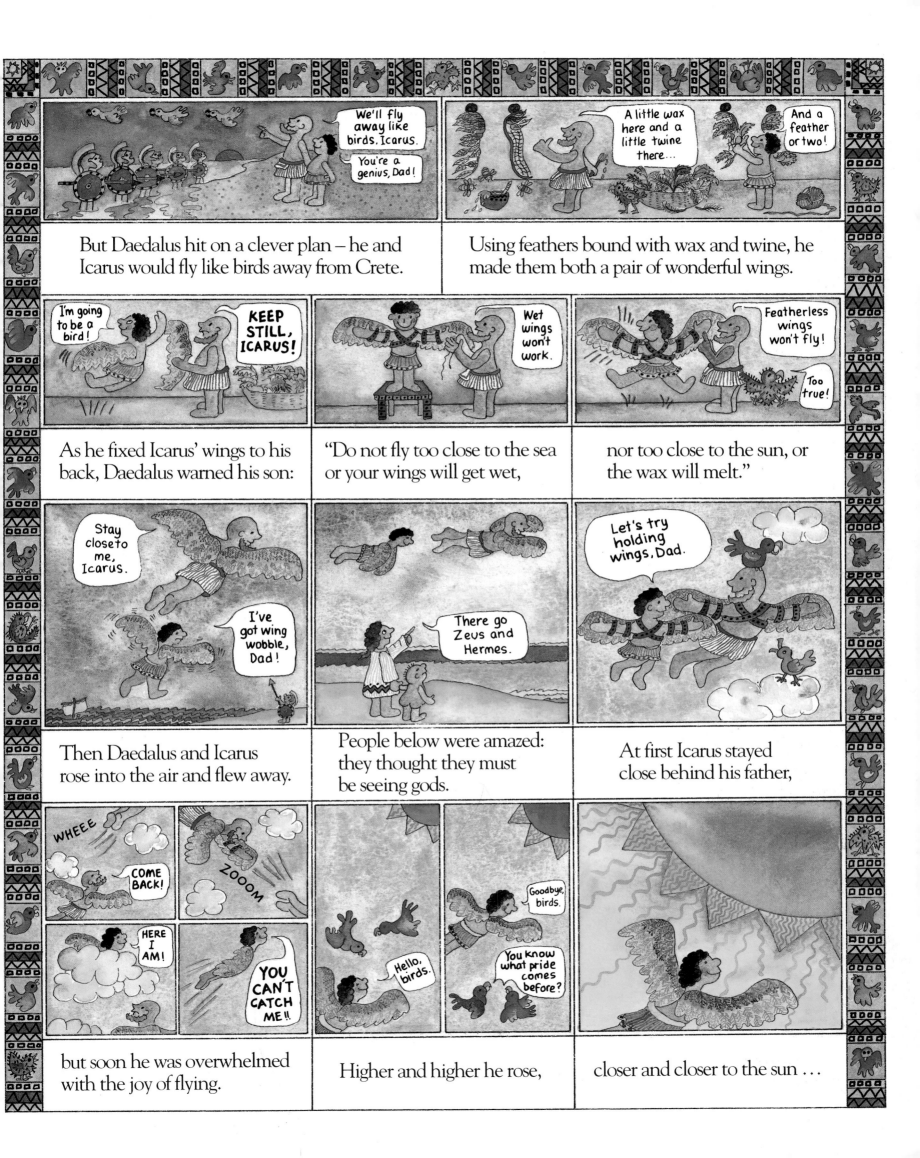

But Daedalus hit on a clever plan – he and Icarus would fly like birds away from Crete.

Using feathers bound with wax and twine, he made them both a pair of wonderful wings.

As he fixed Icarus' wings to his back, Daedalus warned his son:

"Do not fly too close to the sea or your wings will get wet,

nor too close to the sun, or the wax will melt."

Then Daedalus and Icarus rose into the air and flew away.

People below were amazed: they thought they must be seeing gods.

At first Icarus stayed close behind his father,

but soon he was overwhelmed with the joy of flying.

Higher and higher he rose,

closer and closer to the sun ...

until its
hot brilliance
surrounded him.

Then, suddenly, Icarus felt the wax melt. He saw feathers floating all about him.

His arms would not hold up the air and he plunged towards the sea.

Meanwhile, Daedalus had lost sight of his son.

He saw nothing but a few feathers floating on the waves.

He hovered over the sea until Icarus' body floated to the surface.

Weeping, Daedalus carried his dead son to an island,

where he gently laid the body in a grave.

As Daedalus smoothed the earth, a partridge landed by him.

Daedalus believed it to be the spirit of his nephew, Talos, and he knew that the gods had at last punished him, by allowing Icarus to fall to his death – just as Talos had done.

Medusa was one of three monstrous sisters, with brass hands and golden wings, whose glance could turn men and beasts to stone.

But Perseus was not afraid.

He travelled for many days

but found no sign of Medusa.

Wearily, he lay down to rest.

As he slept, the goddess Athene came to him, bringing him a shield

in which to look at Medusa so that he would not be turned to stone.

The next day he set off again, but there was still no sign of Medusa.

That night, the god Hermes visited Perseus.

He gave him a sickle with which to cut off Medusa's snake-covered head.

Then Hermes told Perseus to go to the Grey Ones.

These three sisters had only one eye and one tooth between them.

Perseus went to Mount Atlas, where the Grey Ones lived.

Creeping up behind them, he snatched their single eye and tooth.

The Grey Ones screamed for them to be returned

and Perseus agreed, in exchange for information.

So they told him he must seek out the Ocean Nymphs.

Then Perseus returned the eye and tooth and went on.

Upon reaching the ocean, he called to the Nymphs.

They hated Medusa and were glad to assist Perseus.

They gave him winged sandals, so he could fly,

a helmet to make him completely invisible,

and a bag in which to put Medusa's deadly head.

Then they directed him to where the Gorgons lived.

There, Perseus heard their rumbling, growling snores.

Looking into his shield, he beheld a fearful sight.

Fearlessly, Perseus raised his sickle high …

and with one mighty stroke, sliced off Medusa's head.

In a moment, he had it in the bag.

As he leapt into the air, Medusa's sisters woke.

Quickly, Perseus donned the helmet and instantly vanished from their sight.

His journey home was not an easy one.

But, after a year away, he arrived at Seriphos.

Perseus found his mother hiding from King Polydectes in the temple.

So he went on to the palace.

Polydectes was convinced that Perseus had long since been turned to stone.

The King was horrified to see him alive.

But before he could speak, Perseus pulled out Medusa's head.

Its gaze immediately turned the King to stone.

Perseus then rescued his mother and, before leaving the island, crowned Dictys the new King of Seriphos.

They sailed for Argos where, later, Perseus accidentally killed King Acrisius, as the oracle had predicted.

THESEUS AND THE MINOTAUR

King Minos of Crete had long hated the people of Athens,

for they had killed his son when he took all the prizes at the Athenian games.

To prevent King Minos from waging war against them,

every nine years, the Athenians sent seven youths and maidens to be sacrificed to

the Minotaur – half-man, half-bull – which lived in the Labyrinth on Crete.

Theseus, son of King Aegeus, was angered by this cruelty.

Bravely, he offered to join the next victims and try to kill the Minotaur.

His father begged him not to go with the others,

but Theseus insisted, and prepared to sail for Crete.

He hoisted a black sail as a sign of respect for the victims, but promised to return with a white sail raised, as a sign of his success.

Great storms battered the little ship on its journey to Crete.

When Theseus finally landed, he found King Minos waiting, with his daughter Ariadne.

Ariadne immediately fell madly in love with Theseus,

and she resolved to save him from the Minotaur and marry him.

That night, Ariadne crept softly past the guards.

She gave Theseus a sword, and a ball of magic thread to guide him out of the maze.

Next day, the Athenians were thrown into the Labyrinth.

Once inside, Theseus tied one end of the thread to the door and set off in search of the Minotaur.

The Labyrinth was a confusing maze of cold, dark passages.

Some led nowhere.

Others took him deeper into the maze.

The roar of the Minotaur grew louder.

ROAR!

Suddenly, Theseus came face to face with the hideous monster.

The struggle was long and fierce, for the Minotaur was enormously strong.

But Theseus eventually drove his sword through its heart and it sank to the ground – dead.

Following the thread, Theseus traced his path back to the entrance of the Labyrinth.

Hearing the cheers of Theseus' friends, Ariadne quickly unlocked the door.

Then everyone ran for the ship and set sail for Athens.

After a few days, they stopped at an island, where Ariadne fell asleep.

Theseus, unwilling to marry his enemy's daughter, left her sleeping on the sand.

In all this excitement, Theseus forgot to change his sail from black to white.

Meanwhile, his father, King Aegeus, watched anxiously for his ship.

Sighting the black sail, and thinking the worst, he cast himself on to the rocks below.

As Athenian parents celebrated their children's return, Theseus mourned the death of his father.

So the sad, but heroic Theseus became King of Athens and lived to win many more victories.

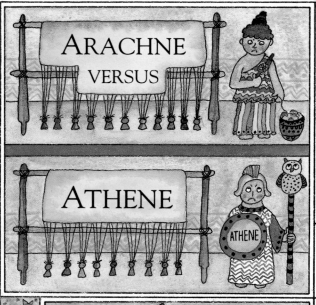

ARACHNE
VERSUS

ATHENE

Arachne lived with her father
in a poor Greek village.

She was not a very beautiful
girl, or a very nice one.

But she was brilliant at weaving,
probably better than anyone else
in Greece.

Arachne certainly thought so,
and never tired of telling others.

Many people thought that her
skill must have been learned
from the great goddess, Athene.

But the arrogant Arachne denied this, believing
that she was even cleverer than the goddess.

This boasting was unwise, for the gods were quick
to anger, when humans claimed great powers.

Morning, noon and night, Arachne's
father begged her not to compare
herself to Athene.

But nothing checked Arachne's conceited
tongue. She even challenged Athene
to a weaving contest.

Soon afterwards, an ugly old woman came to Arachne.

She told Arachne to withdraw her challenge to Athene.

Arachne laughed, declaring that she could out-weave anyone.

The old woman quivered from head to toe with rage, until suddenly …

she was transformed into her true self – the all-powerful goddess, Athene.

Even then the foolish Arachne was unafraid. Athene decided, therefore, to teach her a lesson.

So two looms were set side by side and the amazing contest began.

All day the shuttles flashed back and forth, weaving designs in marvellous colours.

Athene's cloth depicted the gods in all their glory.

But Arachne's cloth showed the gods as drunken fools.

When the sun went down, and the last threads had been woven, the contest ended.

Athene turned to look at Arachne's work.

It was indeed quite perfect, almost as perfect as her own.

But when Athene saw Arachne's insult to the gods, she exploded.

Taking up her shuttle, she slashed Arachne's cloth in two.

Then, turning on Arachne, she beat her about the head.

Even Arachne was awed by such fury. Fearing an even worse fate,

she tied a noose round her neck and hanged herself from a beam.

There she swayed, the life slowly being squeezed out of her body.

Arachne's father, horrified at her plight, begged Athene to spare his daughter.

Grudgingly, the goddess agreed to let her rival live.

She sprinkled herbs upon Arachne – and there began a dreadful transformation.

First, Arachne's hair fell out.

Then her nose, ears and legs fell off.

Her arms disappeared, so that her fingers cleaved to her sides.

Her head and body shrank, until she was no bigger than a fist.

And finally, the rope by which Arachne dangled became a fine, silken thread.

Athene had taken her revenge – she had turned the boastful Arachne into a spider!

MORE WALKER PAPERBACKS
For You to Enjoy

Also by Marcia Williams

BIBLE STORIES

"Highly recommended for 4-year-olds upwards, these three colourful books retell exciting Old Testament stories as if they happened yesterday. Lively and attractive illustrations feature comic-style bubbles above simple texts." *Parents*

0-7445-1469-X   *The Amazing Story of Noah's Ark*
0-7445-1788-5   *Joseph and His Magnificent Coat of Many Colours*
0-7445-1735-4   *Jonah and the Whale*
£3.99 each

WHEN I WAS LITTLE

A series of intriguing comparisons between life now and
what it was like, according to Granny, in her day.

"Delightful… Bright, detailed illustrations provide 2 to 7-year-olds with lots to look at and smile about, and the words are both simple and charming."
Practical Parenting

0-7445-1765-6   £3.99

NOT A WORRY IN THE WORLD

"A brilliant book… Marcia Williams illustrates in a very funny cartoon-strip style… She also offers a few solutions, but one of the best is to laugh at your own fears – something this book will help children do." *Tony Bradman, Parents*

0-7445-2375-3   £3.99

**Walker Paperbacks are available from most booksellers, or by post from
Walker Books Ltd, PO Box 11, Falmouth, Cornwall TR10 9EN.**

To order, send: Title, author, ISBN number and price for each book ordered, your full name and address, cheque or postal order for the total amount, plus postage and packing: UK and BFPO Customers – £1.00 for first book, plus 50p for the second book and plus 30p for each additional book to a maximum charge of £3.00. Overseas and Eire Customers – £2.00 for first book, plus £1.00 for the second book and plus 50p per copy for each additional book.
Prices are correct at time of going to press, but are subject to change without notice.